Wayne Gretzky.

KINGS
LOS ANGELES

BY ROSS RENNIE

CREATIVE EDUCATION INC.

Published by Creative Education, Inc.
123 S. Broad Street, Mankato, Minnesota 56001

Designed by Rita Marshall
Photos by Bruce Bennett Studios,
Frank Howard/Protography and Wide World Photos

Library of Congress Cataloging-in-Publication Data

Rennie, Ross.
   The Los Angeles Kings/by Ross Rennie.
   p.   cm.
   Summary: Presents, in text and illustrations, the history of
the Los Angeles Kings hockey team.
   ISBN 0-88682-280-7
   1. Los Angeles Kings (Hockey team)—History—Juvenile literature.
[1. Los Angeles Kings (Hockey team)—History.   2. Hockey—History.]
I. Title.
GV848.L67R46   1989
796.96′264′0979494—dc20   89-38209
                                                                CIP
                                                                AC

THE BEGINNINGS: 1967–1974

The city of Los Angeles means different things to different people. Many associate it with smog, Hollywood, movie stars, Rodeo Drive, beaches, and earthquakes. If it is entertainment, it belongs in southern California. The people in this part of the United States cherish their leisure time and love to be entertained by professional sports. There are more than four million people in the Los Angeles area, and with that many folks, they can support a wide variety of sports teams. There are baseball, football, basketball, and soccer clubs that call this city home. But until

The acrobatic Mario Lessard played six seasons with the Kings.

recently, it wasn't likely that anyone would associate a winter sport, especially hockey, with Los Angeles. All that changed a bit in 1988 when a major star hit the Los Angeles hockey scene.

Although the arrival of Wayne Gretzky drew a lot of attention to the sport of hockey in this mecca of the sun, hockey had been around for a long time before that. Los Angeles and the surrounding area may be known for many things, but few people realize that there are more Canadians in Los Angeles than in any other city in the world outside of Canada. So it is no wonder that a sport associated with long, hard winters is played in a city where winter means a rainy season.

It was actually one of those dislocated Canadians, Jack Kent Cooke, who started the history of hockey in Los Angeles. When the NHL decided to expand from six to twelve teams in 1967, a lot of people were very surprised to hear that two of the new teams would be located in California. Who could think about playing hockey with sunny beaches to lure the fans away? Other doubts were raised due to the high travel costs the club would incur, as most of the other NHL teams were located on the other side of the country.

No one counted on the talents of owner Jack Kent Cooke, nor did they realize that general manager Larry Regan and coach Red Kelly could combine their talents to field a team that was a contender from its first year.

When the first Los Angeles hockey team skated onto the ice, most knowledgeable hockey observers dismissed them as a group of inexperienced players, lacking in talent. The only exception was goaltender Terry Sawchuk.

Bernie Nicholls was a consistent performer for the Kings during the 1980s.

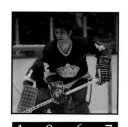

1 9 6 7

The Los Angeles Kings became an official member of the NHL on June 5.

Sawchuk had a lot of previous experience in tough situations, but most agreed even Sawchuk had not faced anything this tough before.

If Cooke was proud of his team from day one, he was almost beside himself when they proved to the other teams they were not a pushover. By the end of the season, the Kings had the best record of any expansion team against the other teams in the league. They had won ten games, lost twelve, and tied two. A sour note, for Cooke at least, was struck when the Forum was ready for its first hockey game on December 30, 1967. But the Kings lost to the Philadelphia Flyers 2–0. Jack Kent Cooke was not a man who took defeat well, and he loudly expressed his distaste for the loss on this special night.

Even so, the Los Angeles Kings made their presence felt. They put together a respectable season with players such as Ted Irvine, Bill "Cowboy" Flett, Lowell MacDonald, and Ed Joyal. In the net was either Sawchuk, when he was healthy, or rookie Wayne Rutledge. With this group as a nucleus the Kings managed second place in the West Division, only one point behind the division-leading Philadelphia Flyers. Both teams had won thirty-one games.

In their premiere year, the team that everyone had laughed at was in the play-offs. Their first performance was impressive, it took the Minnesota North Stars seven games to eliminate the Kings.

The new team had made its mark and would no longer be considered an easy win by the other teams in the NHL. Jack Kent Cooke and his boys had done themselves proud. When the second season rolled around, the Kings were more confident in themselves. Even though the team won fewer games than in their first year, they still were able to qualify for the play-offs by virtue of their fourth-place finish.

The 1969 play-offs brought the Kings their first taste of postseason success. They played the Oakland Seals in the first round, and the contest was far closer than anyone thought it would be. Once more the series went the full seven games, but this time the Kings were the victors. In only their second season the team found itself in the Stanley Cup semifinal series. However, their opponents, the St. Louis Blues, were a far superior club and defeated the Kings easily.

Red Kelly went to work for the Pittsburgh Penguins in 1969 and left a big hole to fill in the Kings' organization. The 1970s would see a string of seven different gentlemen taking over the coaching duties for the team. That alone took a toll on the team, as the lack of consistency behind the bench often led to the same lack of consistency among the players on the ice. With Kelly's departure, the team plummeted to last place with only fourteen wins. This led to four straight years during which the Kings missed the play-offs. Their regular-season record improved somewhat from the dismal results of the 1970 campaign, but never enough to get the team past fifth place in the West Division. Bob Pulford, a former star with the Toronto Maple Leafs, packed in his skates as center for the Kings to move behind the bench in order to see if he could turn the team's fortunes around. That he did.

In Pulford's second year as coach, the Kings qualified once more for postseason play. They faced the Chicago Blackhawks, a team that had moved into the West Division

1 9 6 9

Butch Goring played in his first of twelve seasons for the Kings.

Rogie Vachon was the Kings' most effective goaltender in the 1970s.

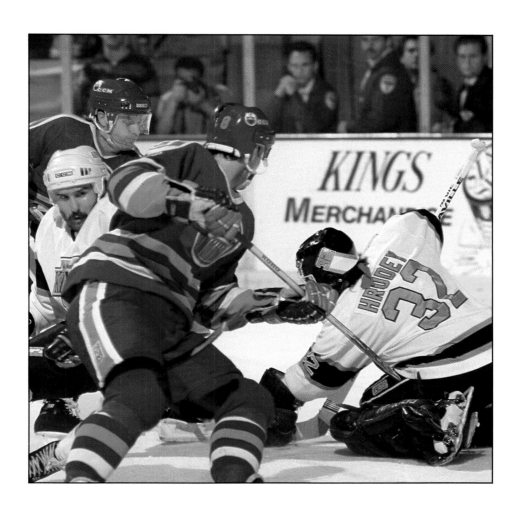

Today, Kelly Hrudey is Los Angeles' number one goaltender.

in 1971. With little play-off experience, the Kings nonetheless did themselves proud. Although they fell to the Blackhawks, Pulford had taught his team defense, and it was evident in the series. The Chicago team scored only eleven goals in the five games. The defensive nature of this series let it be known that expansion teams could play the tough and disciplined style of hockey necessary to win the Stanley Cup. That season, the Philadelphia Flyers would prove that true by being the first expansion team to win the Cup.

GETTING BETTER: 1975–1979

As the team entered the 1974–75 season, they were moved to the Norris Division. This division was perfect for the Kings. So many team records were established that year that it is difficult to count them. Among the many records were most points earned (105), fewest goals allowed against them in a season (185), most ties in a season (21), and the team's longest undefeated streak on the road. They accomplished this last feat by winning eleven consecutive games on the road in the fall of 1974. The goaltending of Rogie Vachon was a major reason for the dramatic turnaround. Team captain Terry Harper had never seen such a change in what most folks considered average hockey players. They gave it everything they had, and the results were outstanding.

1 9 7 7

Marcel Dionne won the Lady Byng Trophy, given to the player exhibiting the most sportsmanship.

Even with such terrific results, however, the Kings were only able to grab second place, eight points behind the division-leading Montreal Canadiens. As a result, they ended up facing the Toronto Maple Leafs in the preliminary round, which the Kings lost two games to one.

The best teams make changes while they are at their peak, to ensure that they will remain at the top of their game. That way, teams won't need to rebuild over a long period of time. Pulford wanted to make sure this would not happen to the Kings. So he arranged a trade with Detroit. It meant that team captain, Terry Harper, would be lost, but in return the Kings would receive one of the greatest stars the team has ever seen, Marcel Dionne. Dionne would rewrite the record book for the Kings. In his twelve seasons with the team, he would earn more honors than the team itself.

Los Angeles had a lock on second place in the Norris Division over the next two years. Although never quite good enough to catch Montreal, they were better than the other squads in their group. With great scoring power on the team and good goaltending to back it up, their fans expected that the Los Angeles Kings would make their best showing ever in the play-offs. They would have were it not for the first-place Bruins, a team set on repeating their Stanley Cup victory performances of the early 1970s. Boston extinguished the Kings' play-off hopes two years straight.

The team's problems grew when Bobby Pulford left the Kings before the 1978 season. Ron Stewart took over for a year behind the bench. The team began to slide even though they still had Marcel Dionne, last season's Lady Byng Trophy winner. Dionne finished second in the scoring race in the NHL in both 1977 and 1979, but those outstanding performances were not enough to carry the whole team. The Kings found themselves unable to compile a successful play-off record.

Both 1978 and 1979 would see the Kings lose out in the preliminary round of the play-offs to Toronto and the New York Rangers. In both cases, Los Angeles could not even manage even a single victory.

THE EIGHTIES BEGIN: 1980–1985

If one star could make a team great, then Marcel Dionne should have made the Kings the greatest team in the NHL. He won the Art Ross Trophy as the league's leading scorer in 1980. Actually, Dionne had the same number of points that year as Wayne Gretzky, but Marcel had two more goals than Wayne, which was the difference needed to determine the winner. There was, of course, one reason that the team was not a winner. They allowed more goals than they scored.

The Kings had the opportunity to build a strong team around Dionne at this time. That didn't quite happen, even

Despite Dionne's scoring, the Kings continued to struggle.

though the team had improved considerably. In June 1980, the Kings acquired a winner in the fourth round of the draft. They chose Bernie Nicholls as the seventy-third pick overall. Nicholls would prove to be an all-star in the making as he matured on the Los Angeles team. The Kings were beginning to build for the 1980s and beyond, and they were willing to wait, for a while at least, to make their mark.

When the 1980 season ended, the team faced tough play-off competition from the New York Islanders in the preliminary round. New York, under coach Al Arbour, had developed a stingy defensive style that was too strong for

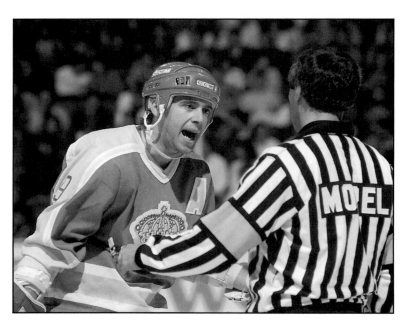

1 9 8 0

Bernie Nicholls and Dave Taylor (Page 17) were major parts of the Kings' rebuilding plans.

Charlie Simmer was a top scorer in 1980 and 1981.

Defenseman Jerry Korab was one of the reasons for the Kings' improvement.

the Kings to penetrate, and the home fans saw their Kings defeated by the eventual Stanley Cup champions of 1980 after only four games. The Kings were denied postseason success once more.

But as the next season unfolded, it looked as though the Kings might write a different sort of play-off story. The Los Angeles Kings set a team record for number of wins during the regular season. They won forty-three games, while Dionne, for the third year in a row, accumulated more than one hundred points during the season. This time there was a major difference in the club. For only the fifth time in the team's history, the Kings allowed fewer goals than they scored on the opposition. They were confident entering the play-offs. Unfortunately, their opponents, the

New York Rangers, were just hitting their stride as they entered postseason play. They came up with great goaltending and, just like the Islanders the year before, they were able to defeat the Kings in four games. It was heartbreaking for Los Angeles. They had put together such a good year only to be eliminated so quickly.

Change can help a team or hurt it. In 1982 there were some big changes that affected the future of the Los Angeles team. The biggest was the realignment of the NHL, a change that was long overdue that resulted in the Kings being shifted from the Norris Division to the Smythe Division. This division consisted of teams that were closest to Los Angeles, such as Vancouver, Edmonton, Colorado, and Calgary. Now at least the division rivals were no farther than fifteen hundred miles away. That may seem quite a distance, but since some of their former rivals in the Norris Divison were over twenty-five hundred miles away, the change shortened the team's traveling time by many hours. However, the realignment also brought discouraging news for Los Angeles. Some of the NHL's top teams were in the Smythe Division. And along with the realignment came another change—the unbalanced schedule. The new schedule meant that teams within a division played each other twice as often as they played the other teams in the league. In other words, the Kings didn't have to travel as far as before, but they had to play the Edmonton Oilers twice as often.

If the first year in the division was to be any indication of things to come, there was not a lot of good news in the changes of 1982 for the Los Angeles team. They took a

1 9 8 1

Dave Taylor established a team scoring record for right wings with 112 points.

Team captain Terry Ruskowski helped the Kings upset the Oilers.

nosedive from forty-three wins the year before to twenty-four wins in 1982. Even with their best efforts, they allowed over three hundred goals to be scored against themselves. It would be years before that statistic would improve.

The Kings defeated the mighty Edmonton Oilers in the play-offs.

If there was any encouraging news, it was the play-offs. The glory was short-lived but refreshing for a team that had not won a play-off series since 1977. By virtue of their fourth- place finish, the Kings played the powerful Edmonton Oilers in the division semifinals that year. The Oilers had finished on top of the division, with 111 points, and were the favorite in the opening series. That took the pressure off the Kings, who played all out. The Kings surprised the Oilers by extending the best-of-five game series to the fifth and final game. The Los Angeles fans had said farewell to their team at the end of the fourth game. They did not expect to see them play in Los Angeles again that year. After all, the Kings were traveling to Edmonton to play the final game, and the Oilers were the stronger team.

Sometimes home-ice advantage can turn into a disadvantage, when a weaker team frustrates the home team and the fans become annoyed. Perhaps that is what happened in this series. In any case, the Kings emerged victorious over the Edmonton Oilers.

Team captain Terry Ruskowski rallied his team for Los Angeles' first attempt at a Smythe Division championship.

The team had given their all to defeat the Oilers. When it came time to face the Vancouver Canucks, the Kings just did not seem to have any firepower left over. The seven-game series was over in five games with only one home-ice victory to their credit. The team had tried their hardest

While Bernie Nicholls provided the offensive spark, Jay Wells played superb defense.

during the play-offs, but it was obvious that they needed to improve if they were to be a serious play-off contender in the future.

Rogie Vachon had retired from goaltending that year and became a part of the Kings' coaching team in 1983. Rogie would eventually become the team's general manager, and it was his job to rebuild the team. That job was a tough one. During the next few years, the Kings failed to make the play-offs.

It was not until 1985 that the club's rebuilding efforts began to reflect in the team's standing. As the team matured, so did Bernie Nicholls, who had been the team's rookie of the year in the 1982–83 season. In Quebec on November 13, 1986, he set an NHL record in a 5–4 Los Angeles victory by scoring a goal in every period of the game, including the overtime winner! In the previous season, he had proven that he was a tough competitor. When his jaw was broken in a game against the Calgary Flames, he missed just two games before returning to the lineup. He played the rest of the season despite a wired jaw. Nicholls would prove to be a big part of the team's future.

The Kings made a dramatic improvement in 1985, recording the team's first winning year in four seasons. Even though they were defeated in the play-offs by the Oilers, the series was close. Every victory was achieved by a margin of only one or two goals. The Kings, for the first time in many years, began to look like contenders for the Stanley Cup.

1 9 8 6

Before joining the Kings, Luc Robitaille was named Canadian Major Junior Player of the Year.

TODAY'S LOS ANGELES KINGS: 1986 AND BEYOND

When Pat Quinn, the team's latest coach, was not able to improve the team's record to any extent, further changes were in order. In 1986 the team missed the play-offs once more. Not only was a coaching change in the works, but changes were made on the ice as well. Los Angeles' superhero throughout most of the 1980s was Marcel Dionne. He had been the first Kings player to break the magic one hundred-plus point total for a single season and had repeated that feat seven times. All of a sudden, in 1987, he found himself wearing a New York Ranger uniform. The Kings had finally realized that building their hopes around one player, year in and year out, was just not going to work in the long run. They needed to have a team with balance.

The fans in Los Angeles liked flashy hockey, exciting plays, and lots of goals. This style of hockey had not resulted in a winner in the city of angels. It worked to a

Wayne Gretzky is the NHL's all-time leading scorer. (pages 26–27)

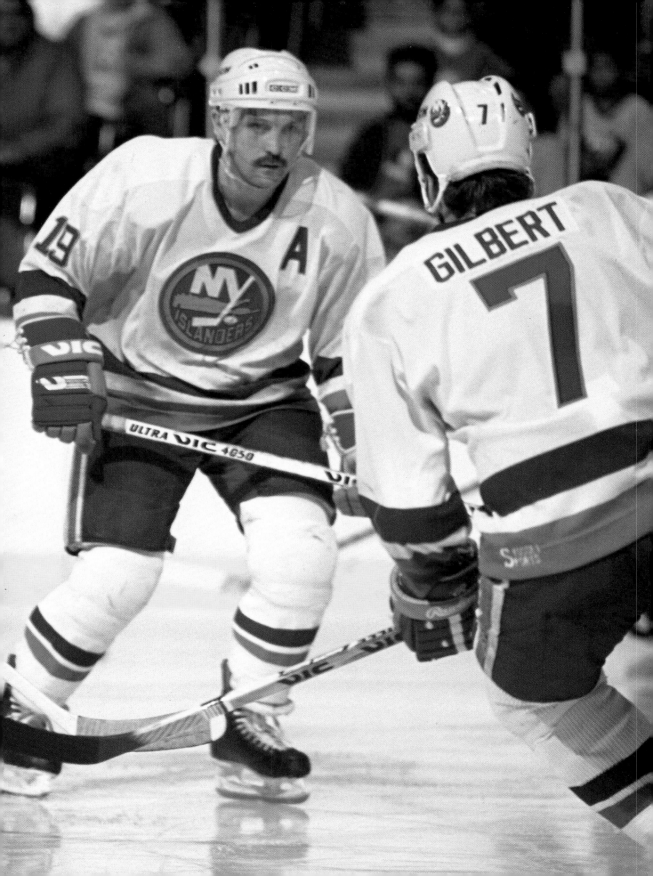

Forward Bob Carpenter was acquired by Los Angeles in a trade with the New York Rangers.

certain extent, but had it not been for a weak Vancouver team in 1987 and 1988, the Kings would not have made it to the play-offs those seasons. As it was, they vanished quickly in the division semifinals against Edmonton and Calgary. The scores were high, the games exciting, but the outcome was not in the Kings' favor. Something had to be done.

On August 9, 1988 something was done—something that would shape the future not only of the Los Angeles Kings but of the entire league as well. On that day, it was announced that the superstar of hockey, Wayne Gretzky, had been traded to the Los Angeles Kings. The news shocked the hockey world. It was hard for many to believe that Gretzky would leave the Edmonton Oilers and his native Canada to come play in Los Angeles, California. But it was true. Gretzky bade a sad farewell to Edmonton and then greeted Los Angeles with a smile. The "King of Hockey" was now a King! Rogie Vachon, commenting on the unbelievable news, said to Kings' owner Bruce McNall, "Thanks for making my job a whole lot easier!"

Gretzky had been the Oilers' all-time leader in games played, goals, assists, and total points. In each of his previous nine seasons in the NHL, he had scored over one hundred points. Wayne ranked first among the league's all-time assist leaders and was third, behind only Gordie Howe and Marcel Dionne, on the all-time scoring list. He was undeniably the premier player of his time, and perhaps of all time.

Gretzky made an immediate impact on the Kings. In the season opener against the Detroit Red Wings, Wayne got his first goal as a Los Angeles King and led his team to victory. As part of the deal, Gretzky had become, if he wasn't already, a multimillionaire. The team had become a winner. The turnaround was dramatic to say the least.

With Gretzky and Bernie Nicholls on the team, the Kings scored more goals than any other team in the NHL during the 1988–89 season. Their point total was an incredible 367 points. For the first time in the team's history, they had two players who had ended the regular season with more than 100 points, Gretzky and Nicholls. And Luc Robitaille just missed the mark with 98.

1   9   8   8

Hockey's greatest star, Wayne Gretzky, became a member of the Los Angeles Kings.

The fans in Los Angeles came in large numbers to see the stars of the hockey world. They hoped Wayne Gretzky would lead the team to its ultimate goal—the Stanley Cup championship.

As if drawn up by the scriptwriters of Hollywood, the 1989 play-offs started with the Kings playing the Edmonton Oilers, Gretzky's old team. The Oilers and the Kings had been fighting it out all season for second place behind the strong Calgary Flames. In the final analysis, the difference was Gretzky. The Kings had finished in second place in the Smythe Division, their best standing ever in their new division. The ninety-one points they amassed during the season was also their best performance ever in the division. It was not as good as a few of their seasons back in the Norris Division, but then again the competition was a lot different.

Even after a full season to prepare, it seemed odd to see Gretzky up against his former teammates during the play-offs. It just didn't seem right. When the series shifted to Edmonton, the fans there alternately booed Wayne and then cheered when he was checked into the boards by an

Kelly Hrudey was acquired in a trade with the Islanders.

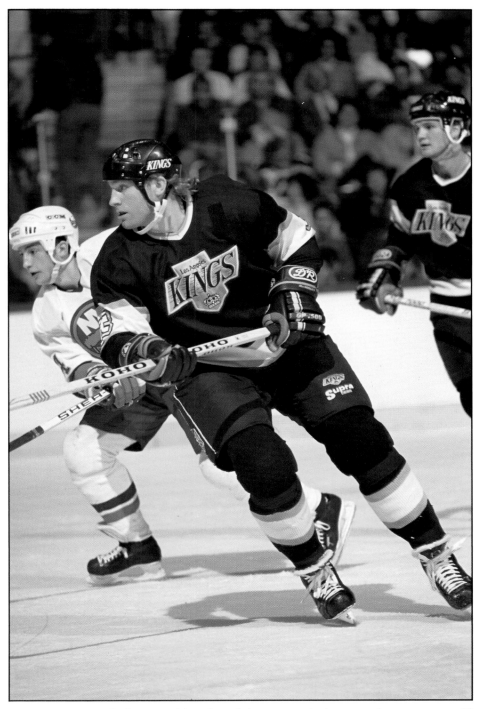

Marty McSorley, one of the talented players on today's Los Angeles Kings. 31

Edmonton player. But whatever feelings of ambivalence Gretzky or any of the Oilers might have had quickly disappeared.

Both teams played hard. Not surprisingly, the Kings prevailed. When the series was finished, each Oiler player lined up to wish the Kings, and especially Gretzky, good luck in the next round. It was the end of one era and the beginning of another. For the first time since the Kings had joined the Smythe Division, they had won a play-off series.

When the history is finally written, Wayne Gretzky may be recognized as the finest player the game of hockey has ever seen, but even the finest player in the world cannot win a game all by himself. Hockey is a team game. It requires a good coach and players who work hard and work together. The Kings did their best against the Calgary Flames during the Smythe Division finals in 1989, but it just wasn't good enough to beat the eventual Stanley Cup champions.

Coach Robbie Ftorek took the blame for the lack of success of the Kings and was fired by Vachon during the summer. The team needed to add some strength to its defense if it was to compete with the best teams in the league during the play-offs. But there was little doubt that with Wayne Gretzky leading the team, the Los Angeles Kings would soon drink from Lord Stanley's Cup as the champions of the league!

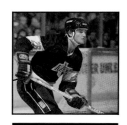

1 9 8 9

Mike Krushelnyski played a major role as the Kings finished with the NHL's fourth best record.